CULTURE
in China

Melanie Guile

First published 2003 by Heinemann Library
a division of Harcourt Education Australia,
18–22 Salmon Street, Port Melbourne Victoria 3207 Australia
(a division of Reed International Books Australia Pty Ltd, ABN 70 001 002 357).
Visit the Heinemann Library website at www.heinemannlibrary.com.au

℞ A Reed Elsevier company

Commissioned and edited by Carmel Heron
Designed by Stella Vassiliou
Photo research by Karen Forsythe
Production by Chris Roberts
Map by Guy Holt

Typeset in Bembo by Polar Design Pty Ltd
Pre-press by Digital Imaging Group (DIG), Melbourne
Printed in China by Wing King Tong Co. Ltd.

*National Library of Australia
Cataloguing-in-Publication data:*

Guile, Melanie, 1949– .
    Culture in China

    Bibliography.
    Includes index.
    For primary and secondary students.
    ISBN 1 74070 131 3.

    1. China – Civilization – Juvenile literature. 2. China – Social life and customs – Juvenile literature. I. Title.

951

Cover photograph of a Peking opera performance in Beijing, China, supplied by Australian Picture Library/Corbis/© Liu Luqun.
Other photographs supplied by: AFP/AAP/Frederic J. Brown: p. 18; AP/AAP/Michel Euler, © 1999, The Associated Press: p. 24; AP/AAP/Michel Lipchitz, © 2000, The Associated Press, p. 23 (left); Australian Picture Library (APL)/Corbis/© AFP: p. 23 (right), /© Bettmann: p. 26, /© Bohemian Nomad Picturemakers: p. 17 (bottom), /© Bojan Brecelj: p. 21, /© Dean Conger: p. 17 (top), /© Langevin Jacques: p. 15 (bottom), /© Wolfgang Koehler: pp. 7 (top), 11, 13, /© Earl & Nazima Kowall: p. 19, /© Liu Liqun: p. 8, /© Wally McNamee: p. 14, /© Tom Nebbia: p. 10, /© Royal Ontario Museum: p. 29, /© Keren Su: p. 15 (top); Austral International Picture Library: p. 25; Courtesy of the Hong Kong Tourism Board: pp. 9, 16, 20; PhotoDisc, pp: 4, 12; *Dragon Bride* by Jiang Tiefeng: 33.25" x 33.25" serigraph on canvas. Published and copyrighted by Fingerhut Group Publisher, Inc., © 1998: p. 28.

Every attempt has been made to trace and acknowledge copyright. Where an attempt has been unsuccessful, the publisher would be pleased to hear from the copyright owner so any omission or error can be rectified.

Disclaimer
Any Internet addresses (URLs) given in this book were valid at the time of printing. However, due to the dynamic nature of the Internet, some addresses may have changed, or sites may have ceased to exist since publication. While the author and publisher regret any inconvenience this may cause readers, no responsibility for any such changes can be accepted by either the author or the publisher.

CONTENTS

Words that appear in bold, **like this**, are explained in the glossary on page 30.

The Middle Kingdom

China is a huge country that sprawls across the world map from Europe to the Pacific Ocean. With 1.27 billion people (one-fifth of the world's population) and a culture that goes back 5000 years, the Chinese are immensely proud of their ancient nation. It is no wonder that they have always seen themselves as the centre of things – the Middle Kingdom.

What is culture?

Culture is a people's way of living. It is the way a group of people identifies itself as separate and different from any other. Culture includes a group's spoken and written language, social customs and habits, as well as its traditions of art, craft, dance, drama, music, literature and religion.

In the centuries since the first **dynasties** (ruling families) emerged around 2200 BC, China developed sophisticated scientific knowledge much earlier than in many other parts of the world. The Chinese built fine cities, canal systems for transport, and raised the Great Wall to keep enemies out. They invented the world's first writing, paper and printing. They knew the Earth was round by AD 139 and used the compass to explore as far as India and Europe. Three of the world's most influential religions – **Taoism**, **Confucianism** and **Buddhism** – emphasised the importance of harmony, obedience and self-discipline. Duty was to the family, the country and its leaders. All this provided a firm and stable basis upon which the arts of painting, music, literature and drama flourished.

Chairman Mao Zedong, founder of the People's Republic of China, led the country for 27 years. Mao died in 1976 and his preserved body lies in Beijing.

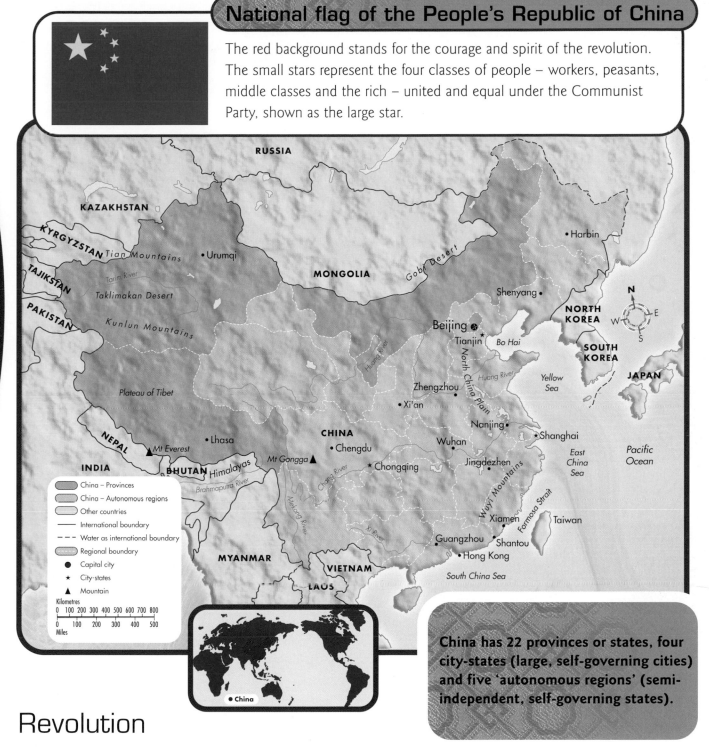

National flag of the People's Republic of China

The red background stands for the courage and spirit of the revolution. The small stars represent the four classes of people – workers, peasants, middle classes and the rich – united and equal under the Communist Party, shown as the large star.

China has 22 provinces or states, four city-states (large, self-governing cities) and five 'autonomous regions' (semi-independent, self-governing states).

Revolution

Over time the Middle Kingdom became inward looking. By 1900, war, **famine**, **corruption** and foreign powers threatened the country's existence. In 1911, the great leader Sun Yat-sen swept away the old emperors and established a republic. After many more years of **civil war**, the **communists** under Mao Zedong took power in the great **revolution** of 1949 and established the People's Republic of China. Order was restored and the lives of poor peasant farmers and workers improved. The **Cultural Revolution** (1966–1976) aimed to rekindle the people's fighting spirit, but in fact it wiped out centuries of cultural tradition in China. Monasteries, temples and galleries were burnt; artists, writers, musicians and performers were killed or **banished**.

After the Cultural Revolution

Since the end of the **Cultural Revolution** in 1976, traditional arts have revived in China. Peking opera, classical Chinese music, puppetry and folk dance are supported with government money. **Martial arts**, acrobatics and diving are sports at which the Chinese once again excel in international competitions. Locally made television series and films entertain the people, and pop music thrives. This activity is fuelled by an ongoing boom in China's economy. Incomes have quadrupled since 1978 and the number of people living in poverty decreased from over 30 per cent in 1978 to under 10 per cent in 1996.

A hard way of life

But the new China is still a poor, crowded, hard-working country. Under President Jiang Zemin and his 2003 successor Hu Jintao, basic health, housing and education are supplied by the government, but the key **communist** value of equality is under threat. Only 30 per cent of the population lives in the cities, but they earn more than twice as much as country people. Young professionals stroll Shanghai's fashionable waterfront in designer clothes, surf the Internet and dance to punk rock at discos. But in the country, peasants plough rice fields with buffalo and live in rustic houses.

Unemployment is rising as inefficient state-run factories close, unable to compete with more profitable private ones. Government **corruption** is a huge problem and **AIDS** affects one in four people in parts of north-central China, due largely to unhygenic blood donor clinics, the sharing of needles among drug addicts and the lack of disease prevention programs. Fifty years of uncontrolled pollution by heavy industry has taken a terrible toll on the environment. Although anti-pollution laws are now in place, nine of the ten most polluted cities in the world are in China. Strict **censorship** of the media is enforced and any opposition is punished.

Caught in the net

In 2002, the more than 50 million Chinese who surf the Internet were astonished when the search engines Altavista and Google were banned, in a government attempt to stop information coming into the country. Many people believe the time of total government control over the media is passed.

Yin and *yang* – the search for balance

Amid the struggle and rush of modern life, people turn to traditions for peace and harmony. Chinese belief says that everything in the universe can be explained as a balance between *yang* (energy, light, maleness) and *yin* (stillness, darkness, femaleness).

Many aspects of Chinese culture aim to maintain this balance. Every morning, people exercise with the slow movements of *tai chi* (*taijiquan*) to prepare their bodies and spirits for the busy day. Meals are prepared with the correct balance of 'heating' and 'cooling' foods to ensure health. Medicine concentrates on the welfare of the whole person, with herbal remedies and **acupuncture** as well as western-style drugs.

Feng shui experts are consulted in the design of buildings to ensure the flow of positive energies. **Ancestors** are especially honoured at Chinese New Year to bring peace and good fortune to the family. Practical and hard-working as Chinese people generally are, they also strive to achieve harmony within themselves and with others.

Ethnic groups

The need for harmony is particularly urgent among China's 55 officially recognised **ethnic groups**. Ninety-four per cent of the population is **Han Chinese**, and Mandarin is the official language, but 70 million people belong to **minority groups**. Many of these have little in common with the majority Han. Tibet was invaded by China in 1950 and strives to keep its own culture and traditions. The Mongolians in the far north-west were historically **nomadic** horsemen, who once conquered the Han. The Uygurs of Xinjiang are not Asian, but **Caucasian Muslims**. Keeping such diverse peoples part of one country takes much military effort from China's vast army.

7

TRADITIONS
and customs

Old and new

Many ancient traditions are still strong in daily life, including respect for elders and **ancestors**, 'saving face' (not being shamed or humiliated), the importance of sharing food after hard work, the love of **tranquillity** in nature and the joy of festivals.

However, the get-rich-quick attitudes now encouraged by the leadership worry some people. They believe the old ways are being swamped by foreign influences and popular culture. Students who fought for **democracy** and freedom in the Tiananmen Square **massacre** of June 1989 wonder at the careless indifference of today's young people. Yet others see this as just another phase in China's long cultural history. As a Chinese saying puts it, 'The one certainty is change'.

Chinese calendar

The Chinese calendar runs on a 12-year cycle known as the Chinese zodiac. Each year is allotted a different animal. The year of the dragon is especially lucky. Here is the zodiac for the current cycle:

1996 – Rat	2002 – Horse
1997 – Ox	2003 – Goat
1998 – Tiger	2004 – Monkey
1999 – Rabbit	2005 – Rooster
2000 – Dragon	2006 – Dog
2001 – Snake	2007 – Pig

Celebrations

China's main holiday is Spring Festival (*Chun Jie*) or Chinese New Year, held in late January or early February. This signals the start of the Chinese lunar calendar, which is based on the monthly cycles of the moon. Everyone celebrates the new beginning. Houses are cleaned, new clothes are bought, debts or arguments are settled, ancestors are acknowledged and family gatherings are held. A highlight of this festival is the dragon dance in the streets when noisy firecrackers are let off to scare evil spirits away and ensure good fortune in the new year. Many people use the holiday to travel and visit relatives, and all tourist spots are jammed at New Year.

At the Lantern Festival (*Yuanxiao Jie*), usually held in February, people make or buy beautifully decorated paper lanterns. When evening comes, they light them and gather in the streets and parks.

Moon or Mid-Autumn Festival (*Zhongqiu Jie*) is a harvest celebration, held in Autumn (September or early October). Special moon cakes are cooked and eaten together with pomelo fruit, a large pear-shaped citrus fruit that ripens in autumn. Fireworks are let off, gifts of mooncakes are exchanged and lovers meet to gaze at the full moon.

Lanterns hung up for Lantern Festival.

Boat racing at Dragon Boat Festival.

Dragon Boat Festival (usually held in June) celebrates the memory of Chu Yuan, a government official and poet who drowned himself around 300 BC in protest at **corruption**. Long rowing boats with richly carved and painted dragon prows race to the beat of drums.

Education

A formal exam system was in place 2000 years ago in China, but schooling was only for the rich. In 1949, the Communists introduced primary education for all. Today, 82 per cent of the population can read and write, which is the best literacy rate in the **developing world**. Children study hard – to fail is to shame the family.

Religions

Under **communist** law, China has no religion, but **Taoism**, **Confucianism**, **Buddhism** and **Islam** are widely practised. Taoism was founded by Laotzu around 600 BC and is based on the idea of *dao* ('the way') – the harmonious spirit of life and nature. Confucius was a philosopher (thinker) whose moral and social laws became the Confucian religion. Buddhism came from India and is based on **Buddha's** teachings on how to reach '**enlightenment**'. Islam is followed by many of China's **ethnic groups**.

Until the late 1990s, all schools and universities were controlled and run by the government. **Graduates** had to accept whatever job the government gave them. Now, students who graduate can choose their own jobs. English is the most popular foreign language studied, and students enjoy practising in evening gatherings called 'English salons' where English-speakers hold conversations with local Chinese.

ETHNIC MINORITIES

China has an astonishing **diversity** of **ethnic groups**, mostly in border regions. There are 55 officially recognised ethnic minorities (around 70 million people). The Uygurs of Central Asia regard themselves as Turkish, not Asian, and are restless for independence. Tibet in the far west of China is a conquered country, and its people generally do not accept Chinese rule. The government now encourages minorities to keep their distinctive cultures after long years of **suppression**.

A Kazakh family having a meal in their *yurt*.

The far-flung tribes

The Kazakhs were historically horsemen who roamed the vast plains of central Asia with their herds. Today, one million Kazakhs live in the remote province of Xinjiang. Some are farmers, but many still live in felt tents (*yurts*), speak their own language and use Arabic script. Kazakhs are **Islamic** and are wary of the many **Han Chinese** who have migrated to the Xinjiang region in recent years.

Over seven million Uygurs also live in Xinjiang. The Uygurs have much in common with the Turks, to whom they are related. They eat lamb kebab and bake wheat flat bread, follow Islam and have their own folk tales and epics. They also have a unique form of opera called the *12 Mukams* – 340 classical songs and folk dances, accompanied by strings and tambourines. More popular, however, are the locally produced Uygur-language television action dramas.

Southern peoples

The southern provinces of Yunnan, Guizhou and Guangxi hold more than half of China's **minority groups**. They tend to stick to their own traditions, though most speak and write Chinese.

The Miao

The Miao are famous for the beauty and skill of their weaving, **batik** (wax-dyed fabric) and embroidery. An ancient Miao folk tale explains their brilliant clothing. A young hunter brought a pheasant home to his mother. Taken by the colour and beauty of the bird, she made a costume to match it. The bird's crest became the tall headpiece, the wings were the richly embroidered sleeves, the tail became the short, pleated skirt and belt, and the legs were the coloured leg-wrappings.

The Jinuo

The 18 000 Jinuo living in the mountains of Yunnan were only officially recognised as a minority group in 1979. They have no written language, but speak Youle. Traditionally, up to 20 families shared large, thatched-roofed huts (long-houses) raised on stilts.

The Jinuo worship nature and the sun, and pay tribute to harvest spirits in their famous *Echeguo* or Big Drum Dance. They are known for their stretched earlobes plugged with thick bamboo sticks (or flowers for **courting** couples). Women wear white hoods and black tunics with striking red-and-white stripes. Traditionally, they regarded teeth blackened with pear-tree sap as a sign of beauty.

A Jinuo girl wearing traditional costume.

Ox Soul Festival

Oxen are the working animals of the Zhuang people of Guangxi, but not at Ox Soul Festival. On this birthday of the Ox King, all oxen are rested and fed on steamed black rice to ensure a good harvest. The Zhuang are the original **indigenous** people of Guangxi and have a rich culture of song and dance.

WOMEN AND GIRLS

The **Confucian** religion taught that women and girls should be obedient to husbands and fathers, and throughout Chinese history women have been second to men. Wife-selling and arranged marriages were common. From ancient times until the 1911 **revolution** of Sun Yat-sen, upper-class women's feet were broken and tightly wrapped with 'foot-binding' bandages to make them smaller, as tiny feet were considered more attractive to men. Although respected as homemakers, only the luckiest women gained an education or paid work.

Equal opportunity

The **communists** were committed to ending **discrimination**. They banned foot binding, made primary education **compulsory** for girls and boys, and offered basic health care to all. The Marriage Law of 1950 banned men's total control over their wives, and required goods to be distributed equally to divorcing couples. Women were expected to do paid work, and senior jobs were given to them. Under the communists, women's lives improved, although the most powerful jobs and roles were still in men's hands.

Women and girls today

The position of women and girls is still not equal. Women's salaries are only 77 per cent of men's and they work mostly in poor, low-status jobs. They are also twice as likely to be unemployed as men.

The communists improved the lot of women by making schooling compulsory for girls.

Although nine years of school are compulsory, many country girls (particularly among **ethnic groups**) are kept home to help on the farms. Whilst 82 per cent of males can read and write, only 62 per cent of females can, and women hold only 25 per cent of university places. Everywhere in China, fathers still lead the family unit and make most decisions, although wives have a strong influence in household matters.

One Child Policy

Launched by Deng Xiaoping in 1979 to slow the rapid growth in population, the One Child Policy makes it illegal to have more than one child. Government benefits for one-child families include cash, better health care and education. Illegal births are punished with large fines. In recent years, the policy has been softened and most peasants are now allowed two children, especially if the first child is a girl.

Boys are valued as breadwinners for poor peasant families, so couples try to make sure their one child is a boy. Abandoning, neglecting and even killing baby girls has become a problem. This results in too many baby boys being born – on average 117 boys to 100 girls (the norm is 106 to 100). Wives are becoming scarce and wife stealing is a problem in country areas. Young women are kidnapped and married by force. Government crackdowns on wife stealing have proved ineffective.

一对夫妇只生育一个孩子

少生有利于国家,有利于家庭,有利于母亲与儿童

少生

A billboard in Shanghai advertising China's One Child Policy.

Dangerous work

Many poverty-stricken peasant girls migrate to the big cities like Beijing and Shanghai seeking work. City factories are crammed with such girls working 12-to-16 hour days and earning poor wages in terrible conditions. Many end up on the streets. Slave traders also target rural women with promises of work. On travelling to their 'jobs' they are sold to businessmen and made to work without pay.

Little emperors

Under the One Child Policy, many only sons are being born. Over-eating (obesity) is a problem for these spoilt 'little emperors', and ambitious parents are using bribery to get their sons into the best schools, where only one per cent of children are admitted. The policy of enforcing one child per family has been criticised internationally but it has achieved great success in slowing China's population growth to just under two children per family.

COSTUME
and clothing

The Chinese have been making fine clothes since 2640 BC when Empress Hsi Ling Shi first wove fabric from the thread of the silk worm. **Ethnic groups** in China's south-east are also famous for their hand-crafted clothes. Print-making, embroidery, pleating, lace and braid-making are ancient crafts still practised in rural China.

Boys wearing Mao suits and caps.

Traditional dress

The *qipao*, a fitted, silk women's dress with high collar and slit skirt, is regarded as the Chinese national costume, although it was first worn by the Manchus to the north of China. It was traditionally worn with trousers, but in the early 1900s women wore it short with silk stockings as a daring fashion statement. After 1949, the **communists** banned traditional dress and replaced it with the loose-fitting 'Mao suit' and cap for both men and women.

Since the reforms of the 1970s, western fashion has become popular and in the cities jeans and business suits are standard. International fashion shows are staged every year in Shanghai and Beijing to promote young designers like the successful Wu Haiyan. Poorer country peasants, however, still wear traditional cone-shaped hats, plain loose jackets and trousers.

Everything old is new again

Traditional Chinese clothes are the latest fashion craze in Beijing and Shanghai, including silk jackets with braided buttons and embroidery, and the women's *qipao*. This figure-hugging dress was rediscovered when film star Gong Li took to wearing them. Now every city boutique has racks of *qipao* in exciting new colours and fabrics. The traditional *dudo* is a tight-fitting top with a halter neck tied at the back by strings. For thousands of years it was worn as underwear, but now it is worn with jeans by the young, slim and trendy.

Colour coding

What colour to wear is not just a matter of taste in China; colours have important meanings. Red stands for happiness and luck. Traditionally, the *dudo* was made of red silk as it was lucky to wear red against the skin. Blue is the colour of power and favoured by men.

Ethnic costumes

The tribal and ethnic groups in China's south-east provinces are renowned for the beauty and skill of their costumes. The Miao wear richly woven and embroidered fabrics in striking reds, blues and whites on black cloth. Their full pleated skirts, embroidered aprons and decorated hats are a brilliant sight. The Ge are famous for their *batik* prints, made by applying wax then dyeing the cloth with deep blue **indigo**. The Dong of Guizhou are known for their embroidered sashes, caps, ribbons and braids, used to striking effect on black fabric. It is said that the brightly decorated skull caps worn by Dong babies ward off evil spirits who mistake them for flowers and pass them by.

A design by Wu Haiyan, inspired by the bright colours worn by ethnic minorities in China. In 1997 Haiyan won the title Top Fashion Designer in China, and she is also successful in Europe and Japan.

Yi wedding customs

The Yi people of Yunnan make a special wedding costume, which the bride keeps until she dies. For the groom, a pair of trousers are sewn by the wife, but she stitches up the leg openings. At the celebration, the groom has to get the trousers on as quickly as he can. He then wears them every day until the first child is born. Then they are used as a wrap for the baby.

FOOD

The ancient Chinese wise man Confucius said, 'Eating is the first happiness', and eating together is an important part of family life in China. In the north, where wheat is grown, baked breads, **dumplings** and wheat noodles are eaten, but rice is the basic (staple) food everywhere else. Soya in the form of bean curd is eaten throughout China as extra protein. The Chinese invented tea, and drink it (without milk or sugar) with every meal. There are four main styles of food in China, based on the regions they come from: Cantonese, Eastern, Northern regions and Sichuan.

Cantonese

Cantonese food is known throughout the world. The fertile southern coast of Guangdong, the region around Guangzhou, supplies seafood (fish, shellfish, octopus), fresh vegetables and an amazing variety of meats (chicken, snake, monkey, dog). Freshness and invention are important in Cantonese cooking. Food is usually chopped and steamed, or stir-fried very quickly in lightly flavoured sauces. Rice is served with every meal.

The Cantonese invented the *dim sum* meal. Tiny morsels of delicious food are cooked in bamboo baskets and wheeled around the restaurant on trolleys. Diners select dozens of different dishes to try. Chicken feet, pork dumplings, fried sesame chicken parcels and shark's fin soup are very popular.

Dim sum, a Cantonese speciality. *Dim sum* means 'to touch the heart' in Chinese, and the food lives up to its name.

Eastern style

Shanghai and Suzhou styles of cooking have been enjoyed by food-lovers for centuries. The fertile Chang (Yangtze) River mouth and coastal fishing grounds provide abundant ingredients. Clams, carp fish, pork and chicken are stir-fried in subtly flavoured sauces. Fresh vegetables and rice are an important contrast to some of the oily meats, such as eel and duck.

Peking ducks. After they are killed and plucked, the ducks are glazed and the body cavities filled with boiling water. While roasting over an open fire, they absorb the aromas of burning fruitwood. The water from the body cavities is drained out to make duck soup.

Northern regions

Rice will not grow in the cold north, so wheat and **millet** are used to make dumplings and noodles. The northern peoples, the Manchus and Mongols, were once **nomadic** horsemen who cooked their food over campfires, so roasted meat (especially lamb) and hot stews are traditional.

Northern dishes tend to be more starchy and fatty than other Chinese styles of cooking, to provide energy in the icy winter climate. Steamed pigeon with yam, stir-fried jellyfish and, of course, Peking duck (crisp-skinned roast duck) are examples of northern-style dishes.

Sichuan style

Sichuan food, from the region around Chengdu, has become famous around the world for its hot and spicy flavours. Red chillies and other fiery spices like garlic, pepper and ginger are stir-fried with pork and chicken, which are often marinated (soaked) or pickled before cooking.

Anyone for a cuppa?

The Chinese first discovered that the dried leaves of a native camellia bush (*Camellia sinensis*) make a good drink when steeped in boiling water. From China, the drink spread first to India and Sri Lanka (where most of the world's tea is grown today) and then to Europe in the 1700s. Tea has important health-giving properties and is particularly helpful for digesting food.

Music

The **communist** government strongly supports traditional Chinese music, which is taught and performed in academies all over the country. Western classical music is also popular in the cities and many of the world's great classical performers have come from China. Pop music is wildly popular, particularly in Hong Kong, and there is a growing rock and punk culture.

Traditional

Chinese music uses a five-tone scale (not an eight-tone scale as in western music) and its sounds are complex and subtle. A traditional orchestra has four divisions: bowed strings, plucked strings, flutes and percussion (mostly gongs and kettle drums). Among the plucked strings are the zithers, including the ancient seven-stringed *guqin*, which noblemen were once required to learn. Chinese opera is accompanied by a traditional orchestra.

Pop and rock

Cute-girl solo artists and clean-cut boy bands singing sugar-sweet songs are all the rage in Chinese pop music. Andy Lau is a Hong Kong-based singer and actor who has become a superstar all over China. Fei Wang has a quirky, elf-like style and is very popular. She was briefly married to pop star Dou Wei, notorious for 'tricking' fans by lip-synching (moving his lips to recorded music) at concerts.

Cui Jian brought hard rock to China when he blitzed the crowd at a 1986 concert with his song 'Nothing to my Name'. The song became an **anthem** for student **democracy** rallies in the 1980s, and Cui performed in Tiananmen Square just 15 days before the **massacre** in 1989.

A tough-looking rocker in a white baseball cap, Cui is highly political and has often been banned by the government. Punk rock, disco, hip hop and every other type of modern music is played in Beijing's night clubs under the watchful eye of the authorities who disapprove of anything too wild.

High on rock music

China's first outdoor rock festival was held in 2000 in the southern Yunnan Province. The Snow Mountain Festival was organised by rock legend Cui Jian (pictured above), and attracted 10 000 fans. Held at Lijiang, a remote town 3700 metres above sea level, the concert was billed as the highest-altitude rock fest ever. Performers had to take breaths of oxygen on stage between songs.

Movement and dance

Acrobatics

Acrobatics were being performed in China around 500 BC and are still very popular. Drawn originally from ancient folk dances and **martial arts**, acrobatic skills include tightrope walking, juggling, balancing, hoop diving and conjuring (magic tricks). The famous Lion Dance evolved from old rituals. Using props of large, decorated lion heads, dancers roll and jump about in imitation of two romping lions. 'Meteor juggling' involves swinging about water-filled glass bowls on ropes (like meteors or falling stars) – without spilling a drop. Chinese acrobats are spectacular athletes and are trained from earliest childhood.

Dance

The 55 **ethnic groups** in China all have their own folk dances. Generally, they are based on ancient tales and performed outdoors for festivals and holy days. In **Han Chinese** folk dance, elaborate costumes are worn with props, including fans, flags and batons. Movements can be graceful, or athletic and energetic.

China's first modern dance school was Guangdong Modern Dance Company in Guangzhou. It was set up by Yang Mei-qi in 1987 and blends ballet, folk and modern US dance styles. Yang gained official acceptance for modern dance, which is now also taught in the famous classical ballet school, the Beijing Dance Academy.

On the stage

Chinese opera

Chinese opera began about 800 years ago during the Yuan Dynasty (1279–1368). It combines drama, singing, dance, music, **martial arts** and lavish costumes in a unique stage experience. Accompanied by a traditional Chinese orchestra of strings, gongs, drums and flutes, actors play heroes and villains in heroic or tragic stories. The performance is not life-like; movements are formal, and mask-like make-up indicates the nature of each character. Traditionally, men played all the female parts and women were not allowed to perform. Now women opera stars are common and many of them play men's parts!

A Peking (Beijing) Opera performer applying mask-like make-up.

Over 300 different forms of opera exist, but the most famous is the Peking (Beijing) opera. Mei Lanfang (1894–1961) is regarded as the country's greatest performer. He brought Chinese opera to the USA, Japan and Russia, and his skill playing female roles was legendary. His house in Beijing is now a museum.

Modern drama

Western-style drama existed during the 1920s and 1930s in China, but war interrupted its development. In 1952, the Beijing People's Art Theatre was set up by actor and playwright Cao Yu (1910–1996). Regarded as the founder of modern Chinese drama, he wrote classic plays such as *Sunrise*, *Wasteland* and *Beijingers*, which are still performed today. Lao She (1899–1966) is the country's best loved playwright. His work, *Teahouse* (1957), about historical and social change over three generations, is perhaps China's most famous play. Lao She died tragically at the hands of the **Red Guards** during the **Cultural Revolution**.

Rod puppets backstage at a Shanghai puppet theatre.

Puppetry

Puppetry goes back 2000 years in China, and there are three different forms. Rod puppets are worked from below using thin metal rods. Shadow puppets made of finely cut leather are designed to be viewed from behind a lit screen on which their shadows are cast. String puppets (marionettes) are worked from above by the puppeteer, who appears on stage. Marionettes are carved in wood and have up to 30 strings. In the hands of a master, they are wonderfully life-like. This form of puppetry has its own music called 'puppet tunes'. Quanzhou Puppet Theatre, run for 50 years by the great puppet master Huang Yi Que, is the premier marionette troupe in China.

No Man's Land Theatre Company

Hong Kong is a thriving centre of modern drama. Tang Shu-wing is famous around the world as a theatre actor and director. His company No Man's Land produces exciting works like *Millennium Autopsy*, which includes puppets, video and other multimedia techniques. In 2002, Tang directed the Nobel Prize-winning author Gao Xingjian's play, *Between Life and Death*.

LITERATURE

Words of the ancients

Poems and stories have been written in China since around 1000 BC when song lyrics by an unknown author were collected into a book called the *Shijing*. Another collection, the *Songs of Chu* was composed in about 200 BC. These works became the great classics of Chinese poetry.

Classical poets

China's most famous poet is Li Bai (also known as Li Po) (AD 701–762), who lived during the Tang Dynasty, the golden age of art and literature. He grew up in Sichuan in South China and travelled all over the country, writing about the beauty of nature, the joy of friendship and the sorrow of parting. About 2000 of Li Bai's poems survive. His poetry is still very popular and studied in schools.

Du Fu (712–770) lived at the same time as Li Bai and was his friend. He is especially famous for his poems against war, bloodshed and poverty. At the age of 47, Du Fu built himself a thatched hut in the town of Chengdu and wrote 240 poems there. The site is now a garden and poets' museum.

Stories from the past

Novels (stories of fiction of book length) appeared in China in about 1400. They were written in a mix of the classical script used only by **scholars** and the common written language, and became very popular. *The Water Margin* (also known as *Rebels of the Marsh*) is a famous novel written during the Song Dynasty (960–1279) about a group of rebels and their adventures. *Journey to the West* (or *Monkey Magic*) by Wu Cheng'en (written around 1570) is a book based on the life of a **Buddhist** monk called Xuan Zang, who travelled to India. Animal and spirit companions travel with him and their antics make a lively story. The cult Japanese TV series 'Monkey' is based on this novel. 'Dream of Red Mansions', written around 1760 by Cao Xueqin, is a very famous novel about a large, wealthy family in Beijing.

Modern literature

Until about 1900, most literature in China was written in an ancient language called *wenyan* or *guwen*, which only scholars could understand. But in the early 1900s, writers began to produce works in everyday script. Lu Xun (1881–1936) is famous as the father of modern Chinese literature. He wrote short stories on modern themes like the bleak and moody works *Diary of a Madman* and *The Story of Ah Q*. Lao She (1899–1966) wrote about the desperate poverty of Beijing street life in *Rickshaw Boy*.

Punk Lit

Under Chairman Mao, writing was strictly controlled, but today's writers are challenging the grip of **communist censorship**. Wang Shuo (born 1958) is the best known of the new young writers called the Punk Lit Group. He has written over 20 novels, as well as film and television scripts. Topics are raw, violent and tough, with criminals, homeless people and gamblers as main characters. His books were condemned as 'spiritual pollution' by the government and banned, but Wang Shuo has a huge cult following in China. Another writer, Zhang Xianliang caused a storm with his frank novel *Half of Man is Woman*.

Writer Wang Shuo has over ten million copies of his books in print and writes for Hollywood. His film *Baba* received a 'Best Film' award at the 53rd International Film Festival.

FILM
and television

Silver screen

Chinese films were made during the 1930s and 1940s, mostly in Shanghai, exploring the difficulties of life in war-torn China. Director Fei Mu (1906–1951) made the great classic *Spring in a Small Town* (1948), which has been called the best Chinese film of all time. After 1949, the **communists** used film as **propaganda**, and all filmmaking that did not promote communism was banned during the **Cultural Revolution** (1966–1976).

Chen Huaikai was a famous filmmaker under Mao, but in 1966, during the Cultural Revolution, he was publicly denounced (criticised) and handed over to the **Red Guards** by his own 14-year-old son and banned from working for ten years. That son, Chen Kaige, deeply regretted his action, and is today one of China's most famous and successful filmmakers. One of the new filmmakers emerging in the 1980s, Chen Kaige (born 1952) won first prize at Cannes Film Festival for *Farewell My Concubine* in 1993.

His friend, the director Zhang Yimou (born 1950) is admired around the world for his sensitive, brilliantly shot films including *Red Sorghum* (1988) and *Raise the Red Lantern* (1991). His complex, tragic stories made their main actress Gong Li an international star. Many of Zhang's films are banned in China. Tian Zhuangzhuang is also regarded as radical and dangerous by the government. His documentary-style film set in Tibet titled *The Horse Thief* (1986) and his famous study of the Cultural Revolution *The Blue Kite* (1993) are both banned.

Madam Mao

Jiang Qing, Mao Zedong's wife, started her career as a movie actress in Shanghai in the 1930s and 1940s. As Madame Mao, she became hated and feared, and was blamed for the terror of the Cultural Revolution. On trial for her crimes, she put on her last performance, abusing court officials and angrily denying the charges.

Actress Gong Li (left) and director Chen Kaige.

A scene from Chen Kaige's film *The Emperor and the Assassin* (1999), the most expensive Chinese film ever made.

'Kung-fu' movies

Known as 'kung-fu' action movies in the west, Hong Kong films are popular throughout Asia. These adventure movies featuring superheroes with magical powers are called *Wu Xia* films in Hong Kong. Jackie Chan is the best-known maker of these films. John Woo's heroic gangster movie *A Better Tomorrow* was much copied in the 1980s. Woo features white doves in his scenes to soften the violence of the themes.

Small screen

The majority of houses in China have a television. Most programs are put out by the government-run Chinese Central Television (CCTV) and content is strictly controlled. Programs include news, dramas, crime shows, documentaries and light entertainment, but the most popular are the locally made soap operas. Chinese TV does include advertisements, and foreign shows (often censored) are also shown. It was reported that former leader Deng Xiaoping's favourite program was the US soap 'Dynasty'. Cable TV came to mainland China with the foreign-owned Star TV in 2001.

Over thousands of years in China, styles of painting, **calligraphy**, pottery and carving changed very little. It was the artist's aim to perfect the techniques handed down from ancient masters. Self-expression was not as important as tradition, spiritual beauty and harmony. With the end of the **Qing Dynasty** in 1911, contemporary (modern) art was born. However, after the **communist revolution** in 1949, all artists were directed to produce works for the state, mostly portraits of Chairman Mao and beaming peasants and workers. Since government reforms in the mid–1970s, however, a thriving new arts scene has emerged.

Traditional painting

Peace and harmony between man and nature are basic to the **Taoist** religion, and these elements are vital in traditional Chinese art. Simple lines on spare, plain backgrounds are common, and colour is used lightly. Ink and brushes are used on the finest paper (called *xuan*) or silk. Flow, thickness and style of brushwork are very important in Chinese art. Landscapes, portraits and detailed studies of nature (called the Bird and Flower style) capture the beauty of the moment. Most traditional paintings include calligraphy (often a poem) and the artist's seal or stamp.

A Bird and Flower style traditional Chinese painting: *The Five-Coloured Parakeet* **by Emperor Hui-tsung, early 12th century.**

A Chinese calligrapher at work. Calligraphy is a highly regarded art form in China.

Old masters

The first great Chinese artist was Ku K'ai-chi who lived around 344–406. He was a master of human figure painting, although he also painted landscapes. Only three copies of his works survive. The scroll titled *Admonitions of the Instructress to the Court Ladies* is the oldest known painting in China.

Wang Wei (699–759) was a famous poet and musician as well as a painter, and became an artist at the emperor's court. His landscapes, painted in black ink, are admired for their magical atmosphere of mist and water. Several of these survive, including the famous *Villa on Zhonguan Mountain*.

Pan Tianshou (1897–1971) was known throughout the world. He was the first to create huge, bold landscapes using traditional 'splashed ink' techniques and forceful brushwork. His beautiful paintings of birds, insects and flowers are in galleries around the world and have even appeared on stamps.

Calligraphy

Each Chinese character is a kind of word picture, so it is not surprising that the skill of writing (calligraphy) is an art form in China. The 'four treasures of the study' of calligraphy are paper, the ink stick, the ink stone (for mixing the powdered ink) and brushes. The same tools are used for traditional Chinese painting. Many different styles or scripts exist, but all emphasise the flow, grace and flair of the brush strokes. Calligraphy is still a highly regarded skill and is used today on banners, flags, important documents, paintings and in temples.

Modern art

Artists in China have generally had a difficult time since the **communist revolution**. Chairman Mao enforced strict rules about art, and self-expression was impossible. During the **Cultural Revolution** (1966–1976) things got worse. Most artists were banned from working and sent for 're-education' to country work camps. Many were beaten and murdered. Since government reforms in the late 1970s, art has been reborn in China, although the government still uses its power to control it.

Today's masters

Han Meilin (born 1937) is one of China's most famous artists. A sculptor, painter, graphic designer and calligrapher who lives in Beijing, Han is the only artist in China to have a gallery named after him. He blends western and Chinese folk art traditions in his work, and is well known at home as the designer of the red phoenix logo for Air China. He also designed the Five Dragon Clock Tower in Atlanta, USA for the 1996 Olympic Games, and his paintings have appeared on United Nations Christmas cards. Han's massive 4800 tonne, 42-metre-long granite sculpture *Group Tigers* has become a tourist attraction in Dalian, in north-east China.

The painting *Dragon Bride*, by Jiang Tiefeng, is a serigraph – a print created by the silk-screen method.

Fang Fengfu (born 1937) works as a professor, artist and calligrapher in Hong Kong and has been awarded several international art prizes. He uses rich, bright colours to paint traditional designs of flowers, birds and trees, as in his famous *Brilliant Autumn Scenery*.

Most popular in America is Jiang Tiefeng (born 1938). He made a living under the communists by painting **propaganda** posters (including the famous red-faced poster of Chairman Mao).

Jiang is China's best-known illustrator of children's books (including the award-winning *Two Little Peacocks* in 1974), but is renowned internationally for his brilliantly coloured and designed oil paintings. In 1979, he painted the *Stone Forest* mural in the Great Hall of the People in Beijing. The work, painted on six silk panels, took seven months to complete. He now lives in the USA.

Porcelain

Thin, lightweight, shiny pottery called porcelain was invented by the Chinese around AD 200. It was exported to Europe for over 1000 years before the secret of its making leaked out. The town of Jingdezhen in Jiangxi Province has always been the main porcelain centre and source of the famous **kaolin** clay. Today, it has dozens of high-tech factories, a porcelain research institute and museum. Many of China's master potters are also based here. They make reproductions of traditional designs, including the famous blue and white **Ming** style and the delicately handpainted scenes of the **Qing Dynasty** period.

Making an impression

Artist Dai Guangyu is making an impact with his 'performance installations'. In his work *Making Traces* (1997) the artist lies in a paper-lined grave in a Shuangliu cemetery for 40 minutes. The mixture of mud and sweat leaves a print of the artist's body on the paper. Other artworks involve spray-painting apples and rice with gold, and a performance in which he sends 64 empty letters to his friends and mails 64 letters back to himself.

Fine porcelain from the Ming and Qing dynasties. The Chinese kept the secret of how to make this costly pottery for hundreds of years.

GLOSSARY

acupuncture   traditional medical practice involving the insertion of needles into the skin

AIDS   Acquired Immune Deficiency Syndrome – a fatal, infectious disease caught by blood, or other body fluids, from an infected person getting into another's bloodstream

ancestors   people from whom one is descended

anthem   a popular song identified with a group

banished   banned from one's home district or country

batik   decorative fabric created by painting patterns onto cloth with melted wax, dyeing the cloth, then removing the wax

Buddha, the   holy man and founder of Buddhism; also known as Gautama Buddha

Buddhist/Buddhism   having to do with Buddhism, or a person who follows the Buddhist religion. Buddhism is a belief system originating in India and now practised worldwide, though primarily in Asian countries and cultures. Buddhists follow the teachings of the Buddha and strive for a peaceful state called enlightenment.

calligraphy   the art and skill of writing (Chinese characters)

Capitalism   an economic and political system where industry and trade are owned and controlled by private individuals and groups

Caucasian   any of a major race of people, including those of Europe, south-west Asia and northern Africa

censorship   act of preventing people from expressing their ideas or opinions

civil war   war in which groups within a country fight one another

communist revolution   the overthrow of the existing government in China in 1949 when the Communists led by Mao Zedong took over the country and founded the People's Republic of China

communists   people belonging to the communist political party. Communists believe in each member of the community receiving what she or he needs, and everyone working for the community rather than for themselves.

compulsory   required by law

Confucianism   religion based on the ideas of the ancient Chinese wise man, Confucius

corruption   unethical or criminal activities by government officials or other powerful people

courting   dating

Cultural Revolution   (1966–1976) a campaign by Communist Party Chairman Mao to get rid of his enemies and enforce the strict attitudes and values of the revolution. Thousands of artists, teachers and writers were killed, tortured or imprisoned by the Red Guards who carried out Mao's orders.

democracy   a system of government in which representatives are elected by the people

developing world   poorer countries of the world whose economies depend mainly on farming

discrimination   unequal or unfair treatment

diverse/diversity   varied

dumplings   small rounds of boiled or baked dough

dynasties   ruling families whose power is passed down from father to son over many generations

enlightenment   condition of spiritual peace and understanding. Enlightenment is the main goal of the Buddhist religion.

ethnic group   people who share a specific culture, language and background

famine   desperate shortage of food; mass starvation

feng shui   the ancient Chinese custom of arranging living spaces according to natural, positive energies to bring good luck to the occupiers

graduates   people who have successfully completed a school or university course

Han Chinese   the largest of China's ethnic groups, Han Chinese make up 94 per cent of the population of China

indigenous   native to a country or region; original inhabitants

indigo   blue dye made from the indigo plant

Islam   the Muslim religion, based on the teachings of the prophet Mohammed

kaolin   white, fine clay essential for making porcelain

martial arts   traditional sports derived from hand-to-hand fighting techniques, for example kickboxing, *tai chi* and judo

massacre   mass killing

millet   a kind of edible grain

Ming (style)   a highly valued blue and white patterned porcelain (pottery) developed during the Ming Dynasty (1368–1644)

minority groups   ethnic groups whose members make up a small percentage of the total population in a region

Muslim   having to do with Islam or a person who follows the religion of Islam. Muslims worship a single god called Allah and follow Allah's teachings, which were spread by the prophet Mohammed and are written about in a holy book called the Koran.

nomad/nomadic   tribal people who roam from place to place; without permanent dwellings

propaganda   promotion of a set of beliefs to the public

Qing Dynasty   Period of Chinese history (1644–1911) during which the Manchu Qing dynasty ruled

Red Guards   young students who acted as soldiers to carry out the Cultural Revolution, much feared for their violence and killing

revolution   overthrow of a system of government

scholars   highly educated people

suppression   denying the right to do something; putting an end to an activity

Taoism   religion founded by the Chinese wise man Laotzu, based on the idea of 'the way' – living in harmony with nature

tranquillity   peace; calmness

INDEX